Breaking Out of Debtors' Prison

How to Reclaim Your Identity, Roll Up Your Sleeves, and Build a Prosperous Name

Aaron Maxwell Montague

MBA, MDiv, MNLP, MTT, MCHt, MSC

Breaking Out of Debtors' Prison

How to Reclaim Your Identity, Roll Up Your Sleeves, and Build a Prosperous Name

ISBN (Paperback): 978-1-967006-43-4
ISBN (eBook): 978-1-967006-44-1

Scripture quotations are taken primarily from the King James Version of the Holy Bible unless otherwise indicated. References to the Torah, the Gospels, and the Quran are included for comparative educational purposes and to illustrate the shared wisdom traditions surrounding stewardship, justice, responsibility, generosity, and community.

Publisher:
MX3 Motivational Books
An imprint of Montague Motivational Ministries
Printed in the United States of America.
First Edition

Dedication

This book is dedicated to the builders.

To those who inherited burdens they did not create but refuse to pass them forward unchanged.

To parents who quietly choose discipline over despair because they understand that children are watching more closely than they are listening.

To grandparents who dream of leaving more than memories and hope to leave wisdom, ownership, opportunity, and a prosperous name.

To communities that have endured exclusion, disruption, and economic hardship yet continue believing that stewardship, ownership, and cooperation remain capable of changing futures.

Most of all, this book is dedicated to the children of the African diaspora and to every person who has ever looked at a balance sheet, a credit report, a foreclosure notice, or an empty bank account and wondered whether the story could still end differently.

It can.

Builders prove it every day.

How to Use This Book

This book was written to be read slowly.

Some readers will arrive carrying manageable debt and searching for a strategy to accelerate financial freedom. Others will arrive facing collection notices, damaged credit, foreclosure, eviction, or circumstances that require immediate stabilization before rebuilding can begin. Still others will arrive not because of personal crisis but because they hope to build businesses, create ownership, establish legacy, and strengthen their communities.

Each reader begins from a different location.

The Montague Method begins by respecting that reality.

Readers are encouraged to move through the chapters in order because each chapter builds upon the foundation established by the previous ones. The early chapters address identity, mindset, and the nature of modern debt. Later chapters introduce practical tools for rebuilding credit, eliminating debt, increasing income, creating ownership, and establishing legacy. The final chapters expand the conversation beyond the individual and into families, communities, and future generations.

This book is not intended as a substitute for legal advice, tax advice, investment advice, or professional counseling. Laws differ by jurisdiction, financial situations differ by household, and wise stewardship often includes seeking qualified assistance when circumstances require it.

Most importantly, this book asks readers to approach themselves with honesty and grace at the same time. Honest measurements make intelligent decisions possible. Grace makes it possible to continue building while those decisions begin producing results.

Builders begin where they are.

Then they build.

Disclaimer

The information contained in this book is intended for educational purposes only and should not be construed as legal advice, tax advice, accounting advice, investment advice, credit repair advice, or financial planning advice specific to any individual situation.

Financial laws, consumer protections, lending practices, foreclosure procedures, collection regulations, and tax consequences vary by jurisdiction and change over time. Readers are encouraged to seek qualified legal, financial, tax, housing, or counseling professionals when circumstances require specialized guidance.

References to debt elimination strategies, credit repair concepts, negotiation techniques, budgeting methods, business ownership, investing, entrepreneurship, and community economics are intended to provide general educational principles rather than individualized recommendations.

The author and publisher make no guarantees regarding financial outcomes, credit scores, debt reduction results, investment performance, business success, or economic improvement resulting from the application of the principles contained in this book.

Responsibility remains one of the central themes of this work because responsibility remains one of the central realities of stewardship. Every reader's circumstances are unique, and wise builders make decisions appropriate to their own resources, obligations, opportunities, and goals.

This book was not written to replace professional counsel.

It was written to help readers ask better questions, make more informed decisions, and approach the work of rebuilding with greater clarity, confidence, and purpose.

Foreword

Some books arrive to answer questions. Others arrive to ask better ones. Breaking Out of Debtors' Prison does both. It enters a conversation that has too often been reduced to balances, interest rates, payment schedules, and credit scores and reminds us that financial struggle is rarely confined to mathematics alone. Debt influences opportunity, health, confidence, relationships, and the stories individuals and families tell themselves about what remains possible for their future.

Aaron Maxwell Montague understands this reality well. Drawing from decades of military service, veterans advocacy, ministry, leadership, coaching, and community engagement, he approaches financial freedom not simply as an economic objective but as an act of restoration. Throughout these pages, readers are invited to reconsider assumptions that may have quietly governed their decisions for years and to see themselves not as prisoners of circumstance but as builders capable of creating new outcomes through stewardship, discipline, ownership, and purposeful action.

As an educator and student of leadership, I was particularly drawn to the interdisciplinary nature of this work. Aaron brings together economics, history, theology, leadership studies, community development, and human behavior in ways that feel practical, accessible, and deeply human. The result is not merely another personal finance book. It is a thoughtful exploration of identity, responsibility, agency, and legacy expressed through the language of stewardship and construction.

The emphasis on the African diaspora is equally important. History matters because it influences access, opportunity, and starting positions in ways that cannot be ignored honestly. Yet this book refuses to surrender the future to the past. Instead, it offers a compelling vision of ownership, institution building, intergenerational responsibility, and community stewardship capable of strengthening families and neighborhoods for decades to come.

One of the strengths of this work is its refusal to promise shortcuts or overnight transformation. The reader will not find formulas for instant wealth or easy success hidden in these pages. What they will find is something far more durable: a method. They will encounter practical tools, disciplined thinking, and a framework through which they can begin reclaiming authorship over their own economic stories.

The book's central insight may also be its most important one. Financial freedom is not the destination. Financial freedom creates the conditions under which larger work becomes possible. Ownership, generosity, stewardship, legacy, and community investment all require room to breathe and resources with which to build. Debt elimination creates that room, but the purpose of the room is construction.

As both an educator and someone who has personally engaged many of the principles explored in this book, I have seen the power of intentional reflection, disciplined action, and consistent effort over time. Transformation rarely arrives dramatically. More often, it appears quietly through decisions repeated often enough that they become habits, habits sustained long enough that they become momentum, and momentum carried far enough that it eventually changes outcomes.

Readers will come to this work from many different places. Some will arrive carrying debt. Others will be rebuilding credit or recovering from financial setbacks that continue casting long shadows over the present. Still others will come seeking wisdom about ownership, stewardship, or legacy. Wherever the journey begins, this book offers both practical guidance and a larger vision of what can be built when people refuse to allow present circumstances to become permanent definitions.

If you have ever wondered whether your financial story can still end differently, these pages offer a thoughtful and hopeful answer. They remind us that while burdens may be real and obstacles may be significant, the future remains unwritten and the builder remains capable of building.

I invite you to read carefully, reflect honestly, and approach the work ahead with both courage and patience. The journey begins not with perfection but with the decision to begin, and builders have always understood that every meaningful structure starts with a single stone placed intentionally upon another.

—Dr. Crystal E. Montague-Lanham, Ed.D.
Interdisciplinary Doctor of Education Leadership

Preface

The strange thing about modern debtors' prison is that the doors are often unlocked, and yet millions of people still feel unable to leave.

The prison is rarely constructed from iron bars or stone walls. More often it is built from minimum payments, collection notices, financial anxiety, damaged credit, postponed dreams, and the quiet exhaustion that comes from watching tomorrow's labor arrive already assigned to yesterday's decisions.

For many people, debt gradually stops feeling like a financial condition and starts feeling like an identity.

That may be its greatest deception.

This book was written because I have spent a lifetime watching good people carry burdens that eventually convinced them they were broken, irresponsible, incapable, or destined to struggle forever. I have watched families postpone ownership, communities postpone investment, and generations postpone possibility because the weight of obligation left little room for imagination.

I no longer believe that debt is merely an economic issue.

I believe it is also an identity issue.

People who see themselves as consumers tend to consume. People who see themselves as victims often learn to endure. Builders, however, approach the world differently. Builders measure honestly, plan carefully, adjust continuously, and continue working long after excitement has left the room.

Builders build.

This book was written particularly with the children of the African diaspora in mind because history has not always provided equal access to ownership, capital, institutions, and opportunity. Acknowledging that history matters. Remaining imprisoned by that history does not. The purpose of this work is not blame. The purpose is construction.

The Montague Method begins with a simple premise: begin where you are, tell yourself the truth, begin with the end in mind, and build patiently enough for discipline to become momentum and momentum to become transformation.

The chapters that follow will discuss debt, credit, ownership, stewardship, crisis management, legacy, generosity, and community economics. Beneath all of those conversations, however, lies a much deeper question.

What should freedom build?

By the time you reach the final page, I hope you discover what builders throughout history eventually discovered for themselves.

The prison may have been real.

The burden may have been real.

The builder is real as well.

Table of Contents

Prologue

The Prison Without Bars

The strange thing about modern debtors' prison is that the doors are often unlocked, and yet millions of people still feel unable to leave.

The original debtors' prisons were easier to recognize. They had walls. They had guards. They had iron bars and heavy doors. Society eventually discovered the absurdity of the arrangement. A person sitting in a cell could not earn wages, support a family, or repay an obligation. The prison satisfied the desire for punishment while frustrating the possibility of restoration.

The walls eventually came down.

The experience remained.

Modern debt rarely announces itself as captivity. It arrives disguised as convenience, opportunity, or necessity. By the time many people recognize its weight, future income has already been assigned to decisions made months or years earlier. The result is seldom dramatic. It is usually quieter than that. A business waits another year. A move is postponed. A calling is deferred until circumstances improve. Entire futures are negotiated with obligations that continue demanding payment long after the original purchase has disappeared.

Debt changes more than balance sheets. It changes the way people experience time. Tomorrow's earnings begin arriving with instructions attached to them. Emergencies become crises because margin has disappeared. Decisions that should be governed by wisdom, purpose, or conviction become governed by due dates.

For some, the burden is temporary and manageable. For others, it settles into something more permanent. The numbers become familiar companions. Minimum payments become monthly rituals. Financial pressure slowly stops feeling like a season and starts feeling like the climate.

That is often the moment identity enters the conversation.

A person who once said, "I have debt," begins saying, "I am bad with money." An event becomes a description. A circumstance becomes a name. The balance migrates from the statement to the mirror.

This book rejects that migration.

Debt is something a person carries. It is not something a person becomes.

The distinction matters because circumstances invite solutions while identities defend themselves. A person who believes they are fundamentally incapable of financial stewardship often treats every setback as evidence. Builders respond differently. They assess conditions honestly, preserve what can be preserved, rebuild what must be rebuilt, and continue construction even when progress is slower than they hoped.

This book was written for builders.

Some readers will arrive carrying collection notices. Others will be facing foreclosure, eviction, service interruptions, or the exhaustion that comes from making impossible choices between competing necessities. Others will appear financially secure while quietly recognizing how little disruption separates stability from crisis. The circumstances vary. The need for a path forward does not.

Financial freedom is often described in numbers, percentages, and account balances. Its deeper value lies in the restoration of options. It creates room for generosity, investment, entrepreneurship, stewardship, and long-term thinking. It allows resources to move toward building rather than merely maintaining.

The purpose of this book is not merely to help readers eliminate debt. It is to help them reclaim stewardship over income, opportunity, and direction. Debt reduction is not the destination. It is the clearing of the ground upon which something larger may eventually stand.

Builders understand this instinctively. They begin with the materials available rather than the materials they wish they had. They study the structure they hope to raise before they pour the foundation. They respect present realities without surrendering future possibilities.

That is where we begin.

Not with shame.

Not with fantasy.

With truth, work, wisdom, and the quiet confidence that builders have carried through every generation:

What can be built can be rebuilt.

Chapter One

What Debtors' Prison Was

Long before credit scores, collection agencies, and electronic payments, societies wrestled with an old and uncomfortable question: What should happen when a person owes money they cannot repay?

For much of human history, the answer was imprisonment.

The practice appeared in various forms across Europe, the Middle East, and the American colonies. Sometimes the debtor was confined until family members paid the obligation. Sometimes creditors paid for the debtor's upkeep while waiting for repayment. Sometimes imprisonment lasted for months. Sometimes for years. The details varied from place to place. The central assumption remained remarkably consistent. Debt was treated not merely as a financial condition but as a matter of personal accountability that justified the loss of liberty.

The arrangement satisfied a certain logic. Debts were promises. Promises mattered. Commerce depends upon trust, and trust depends upon the expectation that obligations will be honored. Societies understood this instinctively. Without confidence that agreements would be fulfilled, trade slows, investment declines, and economic life becomes uncertain.

The problem was not the desire for accountability.

The problem was the method.

A prisoner cannot plant crops, operate a business, earn wages, or provide for a family. Imprisonment transformed financial distress into economic paralysis. The very mechanism designed to encourage repayment often made repayment impossible.

Families suffered alongside the debtor. Spouses lost support. Children lost stability. Communities lost productive labor. Creditors frequently recovered little or nothing at all. Punishment had replaced restoration.

Over time, nations began abandoning the practice. The decision was not merely moral. It was practical. Economies function better when people remain capable of working, producing, and rebuilding. Society gradually recognized that restoring productivity served both debtors and creditors more effectively than confinement ever had.

The walls came down.

The lesson should not be forgotten.

Debt carries consequences because promises matter. A society in which obligations are ignored eventually loses trust, and trust is the currency beneath every economy. The purpose of this book is not to excuse irresponsibility or dismiss legitimate obligations. Integrity requires that debts be honored whenever possible.

At the same time, accountability and hopelessness are not the same thing.

A person facing financial hardship does not cease being a parent, a worker, a builder, an entrepreneur, or a child of God. Economic setbacks may alter circumstances, but they do not alter human worth. The distinction is important because financial distress has always carried the temptation to confuse condition with identity.

The abolition of debtors' prisons represented more than legal reform. It represented a recognition that people are more valuable than their worst financial season.

The irony is that while society dismantled the buildings, many people continue to experience something remarkably similar to the old confinement. The walls are gone. The guards are gone. Yet postponed opportunities, constrained choices, and obligations attached to future earnings continue to produce a familiar feeling.

History removed the prison.

The next chapter asks whether the experience ever truly disappeared.

Chapter Two

What Debtors' Prison Is Today

Modern debtors' prison rarely announces itself with drama. There are no iron bars, no guards walking the perimeter, and no government official arriving to take possession of a person's freedom. The modern version is quieter. It is often mistaken for ordinary life.

It appears in the promotion that cannot be accepted because relocation would be too expensive. It appears in the business that remains a notebook full of ideas because capital is already committed elsewhere. It appears when education, training, travel, or investment are postponed until a future season that never quite seems to arrive.

The mathematics of debt are straightforward. Its influence on decision-making is more difficult to measure. Income that has already been promised elsewhere changes the range of available choices. A household carrying significant obligations may still function, still work hard, and still meet its responsibilities, while quietly discovering that flexibility has become increasingly rare.

Debt also changes the way people experience time. Future earnings begin arriving with prior commitments attached to them. Raises disappear before they are received. Tax refunds arrive already assigned to emergencies that occurred months earlier. Financial progress sometimes feels less like forward movement and more like running hard simply to remain in place.

This reality affects more than budgets. It affects risk tolerance. Entrepreneurship becomes more difficult when failure carries consequences for housing, transportation, or healthcare. Career changes become harder when consistency is more valuable than opportunity. Creativity often struggles to flourish in environments where survival occupies most available attention.

Not all debt functions identically. A mortgage that purchases an appreciating asset differs from high-interest consumer debt. Educational investments may create future opportunities that justify present sacrifice. Businesses often require responsible leverage in order to grow. The issue is not borrowing itself. The issue is whether debt serves the builder or whether the builder eventually begins serving the debt.

Ancient wisdom literature observed that borrowers often become servants to lenders. The observation was not intended as condemnation. It was a recognition that financial obligations create relationships, expectations, and constraints that deserve respect before commitments are made. Every obligation deserves to be evaluated not only according to its monthly payment, but according to the options it may remove from future versions of ourselves.

For some households, the burden extends beyond inconvenience and enters the realm of distress. Collection notices become familiar. Unknown phone numbers go unanswered. Small emergencies trigger larger consequences because no margin exists to absorb disruption. Financial conversations become emotionally charged because numbers on paper have become intertwined with questions of safety, identity, and competence.

The tragedy is not merely financial.

Many people eventually stop believing they are temporarily experiencing hardship and begin believing hardship is simply who they are. The distinction matters. Circumstances invite strategies. Identities tend to protect themselves from contradiction.

This book rejects the idea that financial struggle represents destiny.

A family may inherit debt without inheriting the habits that created it. A community may inherit barriers without inheriting permanent defeat. A person may inherit confusion about money without inheriting lifelong captivity to it.

The purpose of this book is not to promise easy exits from complicated situations. Some rebuilding projects require time. Some require sacrifice. Some require painful decisions and difficult conversations.

Builders understand this.

They also understand something else.

A prison door does not need to swing open dramatically in order to change a life.

Sometimes it opens one payment, one decision, one discipline, and one repaired habit at a time.

Chapter Three

Why Debt Hits the Diaspora Differently

Two families can earn the same income, carry the same debt, and live in the same city while experiencing entirely different financial realities. Income matters, and decisions matter, but history matters as well. Economists distinguish between income and wealth because they serve different purposes. Income supports the present moment. Wealth protects the future. Wealth absorbs emergencies, finances education, supplies business capital, creates opportunity, and purchases time for recovery when life refuses to cooperate with our plans. Income keeps the household moving. Wealth keeps disruption from becoming catastrophe.

For much of the African diaspora, participation in modern economic life began under circumstances that limited opportunities to accumulate assets that quietly support future generations. Land ownership, business ownership, access to capital, and appreciating investments were often restricted or delayed during the very periods when much of the modern middle class was being built. The laws changed, as laws should, but wealth has a long memory. Assets travel through families just as surely as stories, habits, and traditions do.

The presence or absence of wealth often reveals itself during moments of disruption. A family with savings, home equity, investments, and access to support from relatives experiences setbacks differently than a family required to absorb every emergency from current income alone. A medical diagnosis, job loss, divorce, business failure, or major repair carries one set of consequences for a household with reserves and another for a household already operating without margin. The difference is not always discipline or intelligence. Sometimes the difference is simply what was already standing quietly in the background when the storm arrived.

Debt frequently attempts to occupy that space. Credit cards become emergency funds. Student loans become inherited educational capital. Automobile loans become transportation reserves. Borrowed money begins performing tasks that accumulated assets would otherwise have performed. The arrangement may function for a season, but debt charges rent for using tomorrow's resources to solve today's problems, and interest possesses remarkable patience.

Long after the excitement of the purchase has disappeared, the obligation often remains. Furniture wears out. Automobiles age. Vacations become photographs stored somewhere in a phone. Yet the payment continues arriving with remarkable consistency, asking the future to continue financing a past that no longer exists. Debt can be useful when carefully employed in the service of building assets or creating opportunity. It becomes dangerous when it is forced to substitute for wealth that has not yet been built.

None of this removes responsibility. Builders accept responsibility for the structure standing before them whether or not they were present when the first brick was laid. A homeowner discovering cracks in a foundation may study the history of the property, learn why certain decisions were made, and understand the causes of the damage. Eventually, however, attention turns toward repair. Foundations respond to tools rather than explanations and to labor rather than blame.

The wisdom traditions recognized this tension long before economists began measuring it. The Torah established periods of release because permanent economic bondage was viewed as unhealthy for both families and communities. The Gospels repeatedly return to stewardship, generosity, honesty, and responsibility toward one's neighbor. The Quran warns against exploitation while encouraging commerce marked by justice, compassion, and mutual obligation. Across these traditions runs a remarkably consistent thread: obligations matter, but so does restoration. Accountability and rebuilding belong in the same conversation.

This book stands firmly in that tradition. Promises deserve respect because trust remains the invisible infrastructure beneath every economy. Integrity matters because every transaction, every business, and every community ultimately rests upon confidence that agreements will be honored. At the same time, financial hardship should never become a permanent identity or a life sentence handed down from one generation to the next. The purpose of rebuilding is not merely to reduce balances and improve credit scores. It is to restore stewardship, recover options, and create conditions under which future generations inherit opportunity rather than limitation.

History influences starting positions without dictating destinations. Families that inherit little can still build much. Communities that lacked opportunities for ownership in one generation can create institutions in the next. Every inheritance eventually becomes a decision about what will be preserved, what will be repaired, and what will be built for those who arrive later. The relevant question is not simply what we received, but what we intend to leave behind.

Chapter Four

You Are Not Your Credit Score

Numbers have a peculiar way of pretending to be more important than they are. A blood pressure reading may reveal important information about a person's health, but no physician mistakes the measurement for the patient. A speedometer provides useful information about a vehicle's movement, but no driver confuses the gauge with the machine itself. Financial measurements deserve the same treatment. They may describe conditions, trends, and risks. They should never be mistaken for identity.

Credit scores exist because lenders attempt to estimate the likelihood that borrowed money will be repaid according to agreed terms. The score serves a purpose within commerce, and like most tools, it can be useful when understood properly. Problems arise when a number designed to assist lending decisions quietly assumes authority over questions it was never designed to answer. Somewhere between the credit report and the mirror, a measurement becomes a verdict and information begins masquerading as judgment.

Many people know the experience without ever describing it aloud. A score appears on a screen or arrives in a report, and the mind immediately begins attaching meaning that extends far beyond lending risk. A strong score becomes evidence of discipline, intelligence, or success. A damaged score becomes evidence of irresponsibility, failure, or personal deficiency. A tool created for underwriting slowly becomes a substitute for identity, and the substitution often occurs without permission or awareness.

Human beings possess an extraordinary tendency to live consistently with the stories they believe about themselves. A person who sees himself as disorganized often finds evidence supporting that conclusion. A person who believes financial stewardship lies permanently beyond reach may interpret every setback as confirmation that the verdict was accurate all along. The story becomes self-protective. New evidence is filtered through old conclusions, and opportunities for growth are quietly rejected before they are fully considered.

Builders approach information differently. When a builder walks onto a construction site, problems are expected. Foundations crack. Roofs leak. Materials arrive late. Costs exceed estimates. None of these discoveries become personal insults or moral judgments. They are conditions requiring decisions, plans, tools, and labor. The builder studies reality honestly because accurate information is the beginning of intelligent action.

Financial rebuilding requires the same posture. A collection account may reflect poor decisions, unexpected illness, business failure, divorce, unemployment, or circumstances too complicated to fit comfortably into a single explanation. A foreclosure may represent a painful season rather than a permanent identity. A bankruptcy may reveal financial collapse without revealing anything at all about courage, integrity, generosity, faithfulness, or human worth. Some information is painful. Some information is expensive. None of it possesses the authority to define the person holding the report.

The wisdom traditions consistently separate circumstance from identity. The Torah repeatedly measures societies by the way they respond to vulnerability and hardship rather than by the hardship itself. The Gospels are filled with stories of restoration, reconciliation, and new beginnings. The Quran repeatedly calls believers toward mercy, accountability, justice, and renewal. Across traditions there remains a stubborn refusal to allow a difficult season to become the final description of a human life.

This distinction matters because responsibility and shame travel in opposite directions despite often sounding remarkably similar. Responsibility begins with ownership and moves naturally toward action. Shame begins with identity and often settles into paralysis. The statement, "This is my problem to solve," creates movement toward planning and rebuilding. The statement, "This is who I am," often protects the very conditions a person hopes to escape.

None of this removes accountability. Builders do not repair structures by pretending damage does not exist, and financial stewardship cannot be built upon denial. Bills ignored do not become smaller. Statements unopened do not disappear. Recovery begins with honesty because plans built upon fiction eventually collapse under the weight of reality. The purpose of separating debt from identity is not to avoid responsibility. It is to create the conditions under which responsibility can become productive rather than crushing.

The language people use to describe themselves matters more than many realize. The person who says, "I am rebuilding my finances," approaches the future differently than the person who says, "I am bad with money." One statement describes a project. The other describes a person. Projects invite plans, timelines, adjustments, and measurable progress. Identities tend to defend themselves, even when they are painful.

This is why financial rebuilding often begins long before balances change or credit scores improve. The first renovation frequently occurs in the stories people tell themselves about who they are and what remains possible. The builder stops asking whether recovery is deserved and begins asking what must be built next. Budgets begin looking less like punishment and more like blueprints. Discipline begins looking less like deprivation and more like the purchase price of future options.

Credit scores matter because the marketplace has decided they matter. They influence borrowing costs, insurance rates, housing opportunities, and access to capital. They deserve attention and they deserve improvement. They simply do not deserve authority over identity, purpose, or possibility. Markets estimate risk. Human beings contain considerably more than risk calculations can measure.

A credit score may open doors or close them for a season. It cannot determine character, measure resilience, calculate wisdom, or estimate what disciplined effort applied over many years may eventually accomplish. Those assets belong to the builder, and unlike credit scores, they generally increase with use.

Chapter Five

Understanding Debt Before Escaping It

Before a builder removes a wall, he first determines whether the wall is load-bearing. Before a surgeon operates, she first distinguishes between healthy tissue and disease. Financial rebuilding requires the same discipline. Not all debt performs the same function, and treating every obligation as identical often produces more confusion than clarity.

Debt is borrowed money accompanied by an agreement. Resources are received in the present and repayment is promised in the future, often with additional compensation for the use of those resources during the intervening period. At its simplest, debt allows time itself to become negotiable. It permits tomorrow's labor to participate in today's decisions.

Human civilization has relied upon this arrangement for thousands of years. Farmers borrowed seed before harvest. Merchants borrowed capital before trade routes were established. Builders borrowed resources before markets, roads, and cities existed to support repayment. Borrowing is not an economic accident. It is one of the mechanisms through which societies convert vision into reality.

The wisdom traditions recognized both the usefulness and the danger of this arrangement. The Torah regulated lending while seeking to prevent perpetual economic bondage. The Gospels frequently employed financial language to teach stewardship, investment, and accountability. The Quran encouraged commerce while warning against exploitation and practices that transformed lending into oppression. Across traditions, borrowing was treated neither as a virtue nor as a vice, but as a responsibility requiring wisdom.

The modern conversation about debt often suffers from a lack of distinction. Productive debt is generally used to acquire or create an asset capable of producing income, appreciating in value, or increasing productive capacity. Business financing, investment property, and educational opportunities that substantially increase earning power may fall into this category. Such decisions still involve risk and deserve careful analysis, but they are connected to the possibility of future production.

Consumptive debt serves a different purpose. It finances experiences, conveniences, or purchases that begin declining in value immediately or disappear entirely after use. Restaurant meals purchased on credit, revolving balances created by discretionary spending, payday loans, and financing arrangements attached to rapidly depreciating assets often occupy this category. The benefit may be real and the enjoyment genuine, but the obligation frequently survives long after the original purchase has faded from memory.

This distinction matters because productive debt and consumptive debt ask very different things of the future. Productive debt hopes to place an additional worker into tomorrow's workforce. Consumptive debt often sends tomorrow's worker back to pay yesterday's bill. One seeks to expand capacity. The other frequently mortgages capacity that has not yet been created.

One useful way to think about debt is this: debt represents the transfer of tomorrow's labor into today's purchase. Sometimes that exchange is wise. A business may borrow in order to purchase equipment that increases productivity for decades. A family may finance education that creates opportunities otherwise unavailable. A community may invest in infrastructure that serves generations. In those circumstances, future labor is being deployed in the service of future growth.

Other exchanges prove considerably more expensive. A vacation eventually becomes photographs. A meal becomes a memory. Clothing goes out of style. Electronics become obsolete. The payments, however, continue arriving with remarkable punctuality, requesting labor from a future that no longer receives corresponding benefits. Many households discover that they are not merely paying for purchases. They are paying for moments that have already disappeared.

Debt itself possesses no moral character. It is a financial instrument, and financial instruments derive their value from the purpose they serve. A hammer can build a home or damage one. The wisdom of the tool is found less in its design than in the intentions and skill of the person holding it.

The relevant question therefore becomes surprisingly simple. Is the debt serving your future, or is your future serving the debt? Does the obligation increase options, productive capacity, and opportunity, or does it gradually reduce flexibility while consuming resources that might otherwise have been directed toward ownership and investment? Builders learn to ask these questions before signing agreements rather than after opening statements.

The purpose of this chapter is not to produce fear of borrowing or guilt over past decisions. Builders occasionally use leverage because leverage, when employed wisely and sparingly, can accelerate construction. The purpose is discernment. The difference between a tool and a trap is often invisible at the moment of purchase and painfully obvious several years later.

Financial maturity begins when borrowing decisions move beyond monthly payments and begin considering opportunity costs, future obligations, and long-term consequences. The question slowly changes from, "Can I afford the payment?" to "What will this payment prevent me from building?" The first question measures affordability. The second measures stewardship.

That distinction may prove to be one of the most profitable financial habits a builder ever acquires.

Chapter Six

Begin Where You Are

Every successful construction project begins with a survey of the land. The architect may possess beautiful drawings. The builder may possess extraordinary skill. The investors may possess confidence and resources. None of those things eliminate the need to understand the ground upon which the structure will stand.

Financial rebuilding works the same way.

Many people approach money with a strange combination of optimism and avoidance. They know approximately what they owe, approximately what they earn, and approximately where the money goes each month. Approximation may be sufficient for conversation. It is rarely sufficient for construction.

Builders work from measurements.

The first task is neither judgment nor strategy. The first task is observation. What debts exist? What income enters the household? What obligations demand attention each month? Which assets are available? Which habits support progress, and which quietly undermine it? Questions like these are not accusations. They are measurements, and measurements are the beginning of intelligent decisions.

The process can feel uncomfortable because numbers often carry emotional weight far beyond their mathematical value. A balance sheet can awaken embarrassment, regret, frustration, or fear. People sometimes avoid opening statements for the same reason patients avoid medical examinations. There is comfort in not knowing, at least for a little while. Unfortunately, information ignored rarely becomes information improved.

The builder understands something important about reality: truth is always an ally, even when it arrives carrying unpleasant news. A cracked foundation discovered early is less expensive than one discovered late. Water damage hidden behind walls rarely improves with time. Financial conditions follow similar rules. Problems named can be addressed. Problems avoided tend to grow quietly in the dark.

This is one reason shame is such an expensive emotion. Shame encourages concealment at precisely the moment honesty becomes most valuable. It whispers that numbers are verdicts and balances are biographies. It encourages secrecy, delay, and paralysis while presenting itself as protection. Builders learn to distrust that voice because they understand that accurate information is the beginning of freedom rather than the end of it.

Beginning where we are requires an inventory that is both complete and honest. Every debt belongs on the page. Every source of income belongs on the page. Every asset belongs on the page as well. Retirement accounts, tools, skills, certifications, relationships, business opportunities, and earning capacity are all part of the inventory. Builders count liabilities carefully. They count resources with equal care.

Many households know their debts more intimately than their assets. They can recite balances from memory while struggling to describe the value they bring to the marketplace. Yet income is rarely created by debt elimination alone. It is created by productivity, service, creativity, labor, relationships, and opportunity. A builder studies the entire landscape before deciding where to place the first shovel in the ground.

Beginning where we are does not mean surrendering to where we are. A map is useful precisely because it distinguishes location from destination. The traveler standing in Baltimore is not discouraged because the map says he is not yet in Atlanta. The map simply provides information necessary to plan the journey. Financial inventories serve the same purpose. They tell the truth about location while remaining silent about possibility.

This leads naturally to the second principle of rebuilding: builders begin with the end in mind. No one pours concrete without some vision of the structure that will eventually stand upon it. The shape of the foundation depends entirely upon the nature of the building being imagined. A family hoping merely to survive will make different decisions than a family intending to own businesses, fund ministries, educate grandchildren, and leave an inheritance.

Vision changes behavior long before behavior changes outcomes.

The parent saving for a child's education spends differently than the parent saving for a weekend. The entrepreneur building a company evaluates purchases differently than the consumer pursuing convenience. The family determined to become debt free begins asking different questions of every dollar that enters the household.

This is why builders hold two ideas in their minds at the same time. They maintain absolute honesty about present conditions while refusing to confuse present conditions with permanent limitations. They respect the facts without surrendering to them. They acknowledge the distance without questioning the destination.

Financial rebuilding rarely requires perfect conditions. It requires a starting point, a destination, and the willingness to continue moving when progress feels smaller than expected. Most meaningful construction projects are completed one decision, one payment, one discipline, and one adjustment at a time. The work may not always be exciting, but remarkable structures have been raised by ordinary people who simply refused to stop building.

The purpose of this chapter was never to produce discouragement. Its purpose was to establish solid ground beneath the work ahead. Builders cannot change what they refuse to measure, and they cannot reach destinations they have never defined. The work before us begins with honesty and continues with vision.

We begin where we are.

We begin with the end in mind.

Then, like builders in every generation before us, we go to work.

Chapter Seven

The Montague Method

Architects work from drawings. Pilots work from checklists. Surgeons work from procedures refined through experience and repetition. Builders do not rely upon enthusiasm alone because enthusiasm has a peculiar habit of disappearing long before the work is complete. Financial rebuilding requires something sturdier than motivation. It requires a method capable of surviving setbacks, unexpected expenses, market fluctuations, and the ordinary interruptions of life.

The Montague Method begins with a simple observation: money problems are rarely money problems alone. Financial conditions often emerge from the interaction of identity, habits, knowledge, environment, opportunity, and time. Treating only the visible symptoms may provide temporary relief while leaving the underlying structure unchanged. Lasting change requires attention to the foundation beneath the numbers.

The first principle of the Montague Method is identity. Human beings tend to behave in ways that are remarkably consistent with their understanding of themselves. A person who sees himself as a steward approaches money differently than a person who sees himself primarily as a consumer. Builders ask different questions than spenders. They are less interested in appearances than in durability, less interested in immediate gratification than in future utility, and less interested in possessions than in options.

The second principle is honesty. Builders cannot improve measurements they refuse to take. Every debt must be listed. Every source of income must be identified. Every recurring expense deserves attention. The purpose is not guilt or embarrassment. Builders inspect structures in order to repair them, not to shame the previous owner.

The third principle is vision. Debt elimination is a worthy objective, but freedom from debt is not the final destination. A person who escapes debt without developing purpose often discovers that empty space fills quickly. Builders require something to build toward. Ownership, investment, entrepreneurship, generosity, ministry, education, family security, and legacy provide direction to discipline that might otherwise feel restrictive.

The fourth principle is action. Plans have value only when translated into behavior. Budgets remain theories until spending changes. Goals remain wishes until subscriptions are cancelled, payments are made, income increases, and priorities become visible in bank statements rather than notebooks.

The fifth principle is observation. Pilots monitor instruments because small corrections made early prevent major corrections later. Financial stewardship follows the same pattern. Spending should be reviewed. Progress should be measured. Strategies that work should be strengthened. Strategies that fail should be revised without embarrassment or attachment. Builders adjust continuously because reality rarely consults the original plans before changing conditions at the job site.

The sixth principle is adaptation. Economic conditions change. Families grow. Employment changes. Illness arrives unexpectedly. Opportunities appear without warning. The objective is not to create a financial system so rigid that it shatters under pressure. The objective is to create one resilient enough to bend without breaking and disciplined enough to recover quickly when disruptions occur.

Taken together, these principles form the Montague Method. Identity establishes the foundation. Honesty provides the measurements. Vision supplies the destination. Action creates momentum. Observation guides correction. Adaptation preserves progress. Remove any one of these elements and the structure becomes less stable than it first appeared.

The Montague Method rejects waste without rejecting beauty. A well-built home serves its purpose while remaining pleasant to inhabit. A meaningful financial life follows the same pattern. Stewardship creates room for generosity, celebration, rest, and opportunity. The objective is not deprivation. The objective is alignment between resources and values.

Eventually a remarkable shift begins to occur. Financial decisions stop being reactions to circumstances and begin reflecting deliberate intention. Purchases are evaluated according to purpose rather than impulse. Debt is evaluated according to utility rather than desire. Time horizons expand. Future generations enter the conversation. The central question gradually changes from, "What can I afford today?" to "What am I building tomorrow?"

Builders recognize that question immediately because it is the question beneath every blueprint, every foundation, and every structure that survives long enough to shelter those who come after them.

The Montague Method is simple to understand, though not always easy to practice. It asks people to know who they are, tell themselves the truth, define what they intend to build, act consistently with that vision, pay attention to results, and make adjustments without abandoning the destination.

The method is simple. The work is not.

Neither, however, is the reward.

Chapter Eight

Counting the Cost and Counting the Assets

One of the more interesting passages in the wisdom tradition asks a simple question: who begins building a tower without first sitting down to count the cost? The question is not really about towers. It is about stewardship. Ambition without measurement creates frustration. Measurement without ambition creates stagnation. Builders require both.

Many people possess a surprisingly detailed understanding of what they owe and only a vague understanding of what they own. Debts are often memorized with remarkable precision. Credit card balances, automobile loans, student loans, and overdue accounts occupy mental space with an intensity usually reserved for immediate threats. Assets frequently receive less attention despite being equally important to the conversation.

The Montague Method insists that both sides of the ledger deserve equal respect.

Liabilities tell us what is owed.

Assets tell us what can be built.

The first inventory therefore begins with honesty. Every debt belongs on the page. Credit cards, medical collections, student loans, automobile financing, personal loans, judgments, tax obligations, mortgages, and money borrowed from family or friends all deserve inclusion. Numbers hidden from the inventory do not disappear from reality. Builders do not improve structures by ignoring damaged rooms during inspection.

The next step is equally important and often more difficult. Every source of income belongs on the page as well. Wages, pensions, retirement income, business revenue, rental income, side businesses, royalties, and occasional work all contribute to the available resources of the household. Income should not be estimated casually. Builders work from measurements rather than approximations.

Assets deserve the same attention. Savings accounts and retirement balances are obvious examples, but the inventory extends much further than bank statements. Skills have value. Certifications have value. Professional experience has value. Relationships have value. Equipment, tools, intellectual property, business ideas, and earning capacity all belong in the conversation because they influence what may be built next.

This is often the moment when readers discover that they are not nearly as poor as they believed themselves to be.

Cash flow may be tight.

Debt may be substantial.

Resources may nevertheless exist.

A licensed electrician possesses assets that do not appear on a credit report. A retired teacher carries knowledge accumulated over decades. A mechanic possesses productive capacity that can generate income almost immediately. A grandmother who can provide childcare may quietly create economic opportunities for an entire family. Markets assign value to these resources whether the owners recognize that value or not.

Builders learn to count everything.

The inventory should also include habits. Some habits quietly strengthen the structure while others slowly undermine it. Subscription services, convenience purchases, late fees, impulse spending, and emotional spending patterns deserve honest attention. Likewise, saving habits, disciplined purchasing decisions, side income efforts, and intentional financial conversations deserve recognition because strengths are often more useful than weaknesses in predicting future success.

The purpose of this exercise is not condemnation. The purpose is clarity.

A physician cannot prescribe treatment without diagnosis.

An engineer cannot repair a bridge without inspection.

A builder cannot design a plan without measurements.

Financial stewardship follows the same logic.

Many readers will discover surprises during this process. Some will find obligations they underestimated. Others will discover expenses that have quietly multiplied over time. Many will find opportunities they had never previously considered. The inventory occasionally delivers unpleasant news, but unpleasant truth remains more valuable than comforting fiction because truth provides a foundation sturdy enough to build upon.

This chapter also introduces an important distinction between net worth and self-worth. Net worth is an accounting exercise. Self-worth is a statement about human dignity. The two should never be confused. A balance sheet can change dramatically over the course of a lifetime. Human value does not rise and fall with market conditions, employment status, or investment performance.

Builders understand this instinctively. A blueprint does not become less valuable because construction has not yet begun, and a foundation is not judged by the appearance of the unfinished structure standing above it. Potential often arrives long before visible results.

Once the inventory is complete, something remarkable begins to happen. Anxiety starts surrendering ground to information. Information begins giving birth to strategy. Strategy slowly creates movement. Movement, sustained over time, eventually becomes momentum.

The numbers have not changed.

The builder has.

And that change often marks the true beginning of financial freedom.

Chapter Nine

Removing Stones from the Backpack

There is an old image that appears from time to time in conversations about endurance: a traveler walking a long road while carrying a backpack filled with stones. One stone may go unnoticed for miles. Two or three make the journey more difficult but still manageable. Add enough weight, however, and the traveler eventually begins mistaking exhaustion for weakness when the real problem is burden rather than ability.

Debt often behaves in much the same way.

Monthly obligations rarely arrive all at once. They accumulate gradually, sometimes over years, attaching themselves quietly to income that has not yet been earned. A payment here, a financing agreement there, a balance transferred from one account to another, and eventually a household discovers that forward progress requires extraordinary effort simply to maintain the same position.

The purpose of debt elimination is not punishment for past decisions. It is the recovery of energy, flexibility, and options. Every obligation removed from the ledger returns a portion of tomorrow's labor to the person who earned it. Financial freedom rarely arrives as a single event. More often it appears as margin slowly returning to places where pressure once lived.

The financial world has produced numerous systems for eliminating debt, but most belong to one of two families. The debt snowball method focuses first on the smallest balances regardless of interest rate. Early victories create momentum, confidence, and visible progress. The debt avalanche method targets the highest interest rates first, reducing the total cost of repayment over time and improving mathematical efficiency.

Supporters of both approaches can become surprisingly passionate.

Builders generally ask a different question.

Which method will keep you moving?

The mathematically perfect strategy abandoned after three months produces poorer results than the imperfect strategy sustained for three years. Personal finance is unusual in this regard because human behavior often matters as much as arithmetic. The best plan is usually the one that survives disappointment, interruptions, holidays, unexpected repairs, and the occasional month when motivation decides to take a vacation.

Momentum deserves respect because momentum changes identity. The person who eliminates one balance begins seeing himself differently than the person who remains trapped in planning. Progress alters conversations within households. Hope returns to rooms where anxiety once held exclusive occupancy. The numbers matter, but the movement matters as well.

Many builders discover that debt elimination accelerates when income receives the same attention as expenses. There are practical limits to reducing expenditures. There are often fewer limits to increasing value, productivity, service, and earning capacity. Additional training, side businesses, consulting, overtime, freelancing, teaching, coaching, and entrepreneurship have helped countless families shorten journeys that once appeared impossibly long.

The inventory completed in the previous chapter often reveals opportunities hidden in plain sight. A retired mechanic may possess skills that neighbors gladly pay to access. A teacher may tutor. A baker may sell desserts. A writer may create courses, articles, or books. The modern economy rewards usefulness with remarkable consistency, though it does not always reward it immediately.

This is one reason builders learn to ask a different question when evaluating purchases.

Instead of asking, "Can I afford this payment?" they begin asking, "What future payment am I agreeing to make, and what opportunities might this obligation prevent me from pursuing later?" The first question examines affordability. The second examines stewardship.

Along the way there will be setbacks.

Automobiles break.

Children need things unexpectedly.

Medical expenses arrive without invitations.

Life has never shown much interest in respecting financial plans.

Builders expect this.

Contingencies are not evidence of failure. They are evidence that the builder lives in the real world alongside everyone else. Progress is measured less by the absence of disruption than by the speed and discipline with which recovery occurs afterward.

Eventually the backpack becomes lighter.

A payment disappears.

Then another.

Income begins arriving with fewer instructions attached to it.

The future slowly stops belonging to old decisions and begins making itself available for new ones.

The process rarely feels dramatic while it is happening. Looking backward, however, many people struggle to identify the exact moment the journey changed. They simply remember discovering one day that they were carrying less weight than before and walking farther than they once believed possible.

That is often how freedom arrives.

Quietly.

One stone at a time.

Chapter Ten

The Language of Credit

Most people encounter credit long before they understand it. A number appears on a report. An application is approved or denied. Interest rates rise or fall. Somewhere along the way, credit begins to resemble weather: important, influential, and seemingly controlled by forces operating somewhere beyond ordinary experience.

Credit is considerably less mysterious than it first appears.

At its core, a credit report is an attempt to answer a single question: if money is borrowed, how likely is it that the agreement will be honored according to its terms? Lenders, landlords, insurers, and businesses use credit information because they are attempting to estimate future behavior using evidence from the past. The system is imperfect because human beings are imperfect predictors, but the underlying objective is relatively straightforward.

Understanding this changes the conversation immediately. Credit scores are not measuring intelligence, morality, work ethic, spiritual maturity, or human value. They are measuring patterns associated with financial reliability. The distinction matters because problems become easier to solve once they are properly named.

Although scoring models vary, most evaluate similar categories of information. Payment history generally carries the greatest influence because lenders place considerable value on consistency. Amounts owed relative to available credit matter because heavy utilization may suggest financial strain. The length of credit history provides additional context, while account diversity and recent applications contribute smaller pieces to the overall picture.

The important observation is not that these categories exist but that most of them respond to behavior over time. Credit scores often improve for the same reason gardens grow, muscles strengthen, and reputations develop. Small actions repeated consistently produce results that appear sudden only to observers who did not witness the daily work.

Many consumers unintentionally damage their credit because they misunderstand the system they are attempting to navigate. Closing old accounts sometimes reduces available credit and increases utilization ratios. Carrying balances does not improve scores despite persistent myths suggesting otherwise. Missing payments by a few days may create inconvenience, but missing them long enough to trigger reporting consequences can create damage that remains visible for years.

The marketplace rewards predictability because predictability reduces uncertainty. A person who consistently pays obligations as agreed eventually develops a reputation for reliability within the system. That reputation has practical value. Lower borrowing costs, improved access to capital, housing opportunities, insurance considerations, and business flexibility all tend to follow from the same underlying principle: trust lowers friction.

This reality creates an interesting parallel with the wisdom traditions. A good name has always carried economic value. Long before algorithms and credit bureaus existed, merchants extended opportunities to people whose character and reliability had earned confidence within the community. Modern credit systems attempt to perform a similar function, though imperfectly and impersonally, by translating patterns of financial behavior into measurable risk assessments.

Understanding the system does not require admiration for every aspect of it. Credit reporting contains errors. Medical crises can produce long-lasting consequences. Divorces, layoffs, business failures, and economic downturns often leave marks that tell incomplete stories about complicated seasons of life. Builders acknowledge these realities without surrendering to them. Information can be challenged, corrected, improved, and eventually replaced by newer information that better reflects present conditions.

This is one reason patience becomes an important financial asset. Credit improvement rarely arrives in dramatic leaps. More often it resembles rehabilitation after an injury or strength gained through training. Progress accumulates quietly before eventually becoming visible to others. The process can feel slow while it is unfolding and surprisingly fast when viewed in hindsight.

The purpose of understanding credit is not to become obsessed with numbers on a screen. The purpose is stewardship. Credit, when managed wisely, can reduce borrowing costs, expand opportunities, and provide access to tools that help builders construct homes, businesses, ministries, and investments. A strong credit profile is not the destination any more than a well-stocked toolbox is the destination. Both exist to support the work of building something that matters.

By the end of this journey, the reader should view credit differently than when the journey began. It is neither an enemy to fear nor a master to obey. It is a language spoken by financial institutions, and like every language, it becomes considerably less intimidating once the vocabulary is understood.

Chapter Eleven

Repairing the Record

A surprising number of people have never seen their own credit reports. They know the score because scores appear in banking applications, advertisements, and financial dashboards, but the report itself often remains unopened and unexplored. It is an unusual arrangement when considered carefully. Most people would never purchase a home inspection they refused to read or accept a medical test they never reviewed, yet millions make financial decisions based upon records they have never personally examined.

The first principle of credit repair is remarkably simple: obtain the reports and read them carefully. Credit scores summarize information. Credit reports contain the information being summarized. Builders work from blueprints rather than rumors, and financial rebuilding requires the same discipline.

Readers are often surprised by what they discover. Accounts may appear twice under different collection agencies. Balances may be inaccurate. Payments may have been reported incorrectly. Closed accounts occasionally continue reporting as active obligations. In some cases, accounts belong to entirely different individuals with similar names or identifying information. Human systems create human errors, and credit reporting systems are no exception.

This does not mean every unpleasant entry represents a mistake. Some accounts accurately reflect difficult seasons, painful decisions, medical emergencies, business failures, or periods when resources simply proved insufficient for the obligations being carried. Builders gain nothing by arguing with accurate information. Energy spent denying reality is energy unavailable for changing it.

Accuracy, however, matters.

The purpose of a credit report is to provide information useful for decision-making. Inaccurate information corrupts the process for lenders and borrowers alike. A builder reviewing construction drawings would immediately correct measurements that were obviously wrong because the cost of building upon bad information is almost always greater than the inconvenience of correcting it.

Disputing inaccuracies is therefore not an act of avoidance or irresponsibility. It is an act of stewardship. Documentation should be gathered carefully. Communication should remain professional and organized. Dates, account numbers, letters, emails, and records of conversations deserve preservation because rebuilding often rewards patience more than emotion.

Some readers will encounter another opportunity during this process. Creditors and lenders occasionally agree to goodwill adjustments, settlements, payment arrangements, or account modifications that improve reporting outcomes while satisfying legitimate obligations. Such conversations do not always succeed, but builders understand that respectful negotiation often produces better results than silence.

Time itself also participates in credit repair. The marketplace generally places greater emphasis upon recent behavior than ancient mistakes because recent behavior tends to be a stronger predictor of future outcomes. New patterns gradually begin speaking more loudly than old ones. Consistent payments, responsible credit utilization, and disciplined financial habits slowly introduce new evidence into the conversation.

This is one reason discouragement can become so expensive during rebuilding. The early stages of repair often require effort long before visible results appear. Gardens behave this way. Physical training behaves this way. Trust behaves this way. The work begins underground where little can be seen before eventually becoming visible above the surface.

The process invites patience without requiring passivity. Builders continue making payments. They continue monitoring reports. They continue correcting inaccuracies and strengthening habits because they understand that stewardship is less an event than a practice. Progress measured monthly may appear small. Progress measured across several years often appears remarkable.

The larger objective extends beyond improving a score. Credit repair is ultimately about restoring accuracy between present reality and recorded history. A person rebuilding finances deserves a report that reflects who they are becoming rather than one distorted by errors, omissions, or information that no longer tells the entire story.

Records matter.

They simply do not get the final word.

Builders do.

Chapter Twelve

When the Phone Rings

For many people, financial stress has a soundtrack. Sometimes it arrives as an unfamiliar number appearing on a phone screen during dinner. Sometimes it arrives in the form of an envelope opened more cautiously than eagerly. Sometimes it arrives in the quiet calculations performed in the darkness of early morning, when balances, due dates, and possibilities begin competing for attention that should belong to sleep. Debt rarely remains a mathematical exercise for very long. It gradually becomes emotional, relational, and physical as well.

The emotional cost matters because fear changes behavior. Statements remain unopened. Calls go unanswered. Conversations are postponed. Problems that might have been manageable in their early stages quietly grow larger while waiting for attention they eventually demand anyway. Financial pressure has a remarkable ability to convince intelligent people that avoidance is a strategy when it is usually only a delay.

Builders learn early that uncertainty is expensive. A person who does not understand rights, obligations, timelines, or available options often surrenders peace long before circumstances require it. Much of the suffering associated with debt comes not from the obligation itself but from the imagination filling empty spaces with worst-case scenarios. Information does not eliminate difficulty, but it frequently restores proportion.

Creditors possess legitimate interests. Money was borrowed. Agreements were made. Trust remains one of the invisible foundations beneath every economy because lending becomes impossible when promises lose meaning. Most creditors are not attempting to punish borrowers. They are attempting to recover assets according to agreements voluntarily entered into by both parties. Understanding this changes the conversation because it replaces mystery with context.

Borrowers, however, possess rights alongside responsibilities. Collection practices are generally governed by laws, regulations, and professional standards designed to distinguish legitimate recovery efforts from intimidation, harassment, and abuse. Builders benefit from understanding these protections because confidence grows when people understand both the rules governing the game and the boundaries within which others must operate.

The first practical response to financial distress is communication. Many lenders maintain hardship programs, temporary payment arrangements, forbearance options, settlement opportunities, and restructuring programs that remain undiscovered because the conversation never begins. Institutions generally prefer cooperation to litigation and repayment to default. The earlier communication begins, the more options tend to remain available.

The second response is organization. Builders gather statements, correspondence, account numbers, balances, payment histories, and records of conversations into one place because decisions improve when information becomes accessible. Obligations should be organized according to urgency and consequences rather than emotional discomfort. A missed credit card payment and an impending foreclosure may both deserve attention, but they do not demand the same response or operate on the same timeline.

Documentation becomes particularly valuable when accounts are disputed, transferred between collection agencies, or reported inaccurately. Dates, names, agreements, and written communication often become important long after memories begin fading. Builders preserve records for the same reason engineers preserve measurements and architects preserve plans: reconstruction depends upon reliable information.

Not every collector behaves honorably, and pretending otherwise serves no one. Some organizations rely heavily upon urgency, confusion, and exhaustion because frightened people often make decisions they would reject under calmer circumstances. Preparation changes the emotional character of these conversations. Builders verify obligations, request documentation when appropriate, communicate professionally, and make decisions from information rather than pressure.

What changes when this approach is adopted is not always the balance itself, at least not immediately. What changes first is often the experience of carrying the burden. Anxiety begins surrendering territory to information. Information begins producing strategy. Strategy creates movement. Movement creates momentum. The circumstances may remain difficult for a season, but difficult circumstances and helplessness are not the same condition.

The emotional burden deserves attention as well because financial distress rarely travels alone. It strains marriages, interrupts sleep, diminishes concentration, and influences physical health in ways that seldom appear on financial statements. Builders acknowledge this openly because difficult seasons were never intended to be carried in isolation. Families, faith communities, counselors, trusted friends, and professional advisors often become important parts of the rebuilding process.

Eventually the phone rings again. The number may still be unfamiliar and the obligations may not yet have disappeared. What has changed is the person answering the call. Knowledge has replaced much of the uncertainty. Preparation has replaced much of the fear. A plan has begun replacing helplessness with movement. Creditors may retain claims upon yesterday's agreements, but they do not possess authority over tomorrow's possibilities.

Chapter Thirteen

When the Storm Has Already Arrived

Most financial books are written for people attempting to improve their position. This chapter is written for people attempting to protect it. There is an important difference between optimization and survival, and advice that sounds perfectly reasonable in one environment can sound almost absurd in the other. A family evaluating investment opportunities occupies a different emotional world than a family deciding whether this month's income should go toward rent, groceries, medication, or keeping the lights on. Builders recognize this distinction because triage follows different rules than construction.

Financial crises arrive through many doors. Illness enters households that planned carefully. Employers close businesses that once appeared stable. Marriages end. Caregiving responsibilities increase unexpectedly. Accidents occur. Economic downturns arrive with little concern for household budgets or long-term plans. Some emergencies emerge from poor decisions, but many arrive through circumstances that no reasonable person would have selected voluntarily. Understanding this distinction matters because shame consumes energy that crisis management desperately requires elsewhere.

The first responsibility during a financial emergency is stabilization. Builders protect the foundation before they concern themselves with expansion, decoration, or optimization because everything else depends upon the integrity of the structure beneath it. Shelter, food, utilities, transportation, healthcare, and access to income deserve immediate attention because they preserve the capacity to recover. Financial obligations differ in urgency, and recognizing those differences allows limited resources to accomplish the greatest possible good.

This changes the order in which problems are approached. Housing generally receives attention before unsecured debt because preserving shelter protects every member of the household simultaneously. Utilities often deserve attention before credit card balances because darkness, heat, refrigeration, and communication influence health, safety, and employability. Transportation that preserves access to work may become more important than obligations carrying fewer immediate consequences because income remains one of the most powerful tools available for rebuilding.

Communication becomes especially important during these seasons. Mortgage companies, landlords, hospitals, lenders, and utility providers frequently maintain hardship programs, payment arrangements, temporary extensions, and emergency options that remain invisible until someone asks about them. Assistance is never guaranteed, but silence rarely improves outcomes. Builders communicate early because options tend to decrease as timelines become shorter and consequences become larger.

Communities matter during storms because human beings were never designed to carry every burden in isolation. Faith communities, family networks, veteran organizations, local charities, food assistance programs, and community agencies often provide support capable of preserving stability long enough for rebuilding to begin. Many people resist asking for help because they confuse temporary need with permanent identity. Builders reject that confusion. A family receiving assistance during hardship has not surrendered dignity any more than a patient receiving treatment has surrendered health.

Documentation becomes increasingly valuable when circumstances become chaotic. Eviction notices, foreclosure timelines, utility disconnection dates, benefit applications, account statements, and records of communication help transform anxiety into action because action attaches itself to calendars and priorities while fear often remains vague and unstructured. Builders move problems from imagination to paper whenever possible because paper can be organized, prioritized, and addressed.

This chapter also requires an uncomfortable acknowledgment: not every problem can be solved immediately. Some debts will require negotiation. Some balances will survive longer than anyone prefers. Some obligations may need to wait while shelter, food, healthcare, and income receive immediate attention. Builders understand that survival and surrender are not the same thing. Preserving strength and resources for the larger battle has always been part of wise strategy.

One of the first changes that occurs during effective crisis management is not financial but psychological. A family that had been drifting begins steering. A person reacting to emergencies begins establishing priorities. Anxiety gradually gives way to information, and information slowly gives birth to plans. The numbers may not improve immediately, but movement often appears long before relief arrives.

Financial crises possess one characteristic that becomes difficult to recognize while standing in the middle of them: they are temporary conditions rather than permanent climates. Employment returns. Balances decline. Communities recover from disasters that once appeared insurmountable. Families rebuild after losses they once believed would define them forever. Builders belong to that same long tradition of recovery, reconstruction, and renewal.

During crisis, priorities become remarkably clear. Protect the people first. Protect the shelter that keeps them safe. Protect the transportation and income that make recovery possible. Above all, protect the possibility of tomorrow because rebuilding becomes infinitely more difficult when today's decisions unnecessarily destroy tomorrow's options.

The purpose of this chapter is not to minimize suffering or romanticize hardship. Financial emergencies are exhausting. They test marriages, health, confidence, faith, and patience in ways that cannot be fully understood from outside the experience itself. They also do not possess the authority to determine the remainder of the story.

The builder who emerges from the storm remains the builder.

The storm never had the authority to change that.

Chapter Fourteen

The Debt Elimination Blueprint

Every builder eventually reaches the same moment. The survey has been completed, the materials have been counted, and the plans have been drawn. At some point the measuring must give way to movement. Debt elimination begins at precisely that moment, not when conditions become perfect, but when decisions begin replacing delay.

One of the more discouraging features of debt is that large balances create the illusion that progress is impossible. A mountain viewed from a distance appears immovable because the eye struggles to imagine the effect of thousands of individual steps. Builders learn to distrust that illusion. Most large structures are assembled one beam, one wall, and one foundation pour at a time. Financial reconstruction follows remarkably similar rules.

The first objective is to create margin. Small leaks become large problems when resources are already stretched thin, and many households discover that subscriptions, fees, convenience purchases, and habitual spending patterns quietly consume resources that could be directed toward rebuilding. The purpose of this exercise is not deprivation. Builders do not remove weight from an aircraft because they dislike luggage. They remove it because unnecessary weight limits range and performance.

Income deserves equal attention. There are practical limits to expense reduction, but the human capacity to create value is often much larger than people first imagine. Additional training, overtime opportunities, consulting, side businesses, seasonal employment, tutoring, coaching, skilled trades, and entrepreneurial ventures have helped countless families accelerate journeys that once appeared impossibly long. The marketplace has always rewarded usefulness, although it does not always reward it immediately.

Once margin begins appearing, a decision must be made regarding deployment. Some households prefer eliminating smaller balances first because visible progress creates motivation and momentum. Others prefer attacking high-interest obligations first because reducing the cost of borrowing improves long-term efficiency. Both approaches have produced remarkable results because success depends less upon mathematical perfection than upon consistency sustained over time.

The Montague Method asks a slightly different question. Which strategy is most likely to keep the builder building?

An elegant plan abandoned after three months generally produces poorer results than an imperfect plan sustained for three years. Financial stewardship operates at the intersection of mathematics and behavior, and behavior frequently determines outcomes long after arithmetic has finished making its arguments.

Momentum deserves respect because momentum changes the emotional experience of rebuilding. The first account paid in full creates evidence that progress is possible. The second payment often arrives more quickly than expected because confidence and competence tend to travel together. Families begin having different conversations about money. The future slowly begins feeling like a destination rather than a threat.

Additional payments deserve intentionality. Tax refunds, bonuses, gifts, overtime income, and proceeds from sold possessions often disappear quickly when they arrive without assignment. Builders give unexpected resources instructions before the resources arrive because money without purpose tends to find purposes of its own.

This chapter also introduces an important discipline: refusing to create new obligations while eliminating old ones. Digging a hole and filling it simultaneously is exhausting work and produces surprisingly little visible progress. Builders protect momentum carefully because momentum is difficult to create and remarkably easy to interrupt.

Setbacks will occur because life has never demonstrated much interest in respecting financial plans. Appliances fail. Automobiles require repairs. Medical expenses arrive unexpectedly. Children grow with astonishing speed and corresponding expense. Builders expect interruptions without confusing interruptions with defeat. The objective is not perfection but recovery, because recovery repeated often enough begins looking remarkably similar to resilience.

The journey eventually produces a surprising result. Income begins arriving with fewer instructions attached to it. Obligations that once occupied permanent residence in the monthly budget quietly disappear. Flexibility returns. Decisions become easier because fewer voices are competing for every dollar entering the household.

The process rarely feels dramatic while it is happening. Looking backward, however, many builders struggle to identify the exact moment the burden became lighter. They simply remember discovering one day that they were carrying less than before and walking farther than they once believed possible.

Debt elimination is often described as subtraction. Builders eventually discover that it feels much more like recovery as time, options, energy, and future possibilities slowly return to places where obligations once stood.

Chapter Fifteen

The Other Side of the Equation

Most conversations about financial recovery eventually arrive at the same location. Expenses are reduced. Subscriptions are cancelled. Spending habits are examined carefully and unnecessary obligations are removed wherever possible. These disciplines matter because leaks ignored eventually sink even well-built ships. There is, however, a limit to how much a household can cut before frugality begins consuming quality of life and restricting future possibilities.

Income operates differently.

Expenses generally have a floor beneath which they cannot reasonably fall. Human creativity, productivity, and usefulness possess no similar ceiling. Throughout history, families have improved their circumstances not only by preserving resources but by creating additional value for the communities around them. The modern economy remains remarkably willing to reward people who solve problems, meet needs, reduce friction, or improve outcomes for others.

This observation changes the emotional character of financial conversations because it shifts attention from scarcity toward possibility. A budget built entirely upon reduction often feels restrictive because every decision sounds like subtraction. Income generation introduces addition back into the conversation and allows rebuilding to feel creative rather than merely defensive.

The inventory completed earlier in this process frequently reveals opportunities that had been hiding in plain sight. Skills possess value. Experience possesses value. Certifications, licenses, hobbies, equipment, relationships, and professional expertise all represent forms of capital that may not appear on traditional balance sheets but nevertheless influence earning capacity in meaningful ways.

A retired teacher may tutor students struggling academically. A mechanic may perform repairs during evenings or weekends. A skilled baker may serve weddings and community events. Writers teach. Coaches coach. Craftsmen build. Consultants advise. The specific opportunity matters less than the underlying principle: usefulness has market value, and markets have demonstrated remarkable consistency in rewarding people who make themselves useful to others.

The wisdom traditions understood this relationship long before economists attempted to quantify it. The farmer plants with expectation. The merchant trades with expectation. The craftsman sharpens his tools because excellence improves outcomes for both the worker and the customer. Productivity has always occupied an honored place within healthy communities because productivity allows households to care for themselves while creating value for others at the same time.

This chapter is not advocating exhaustion disguised as ambition. Human beings require rest, families require attention, and health remains one of the most valuable assets any builder possesses. The objective is not endless labor but intentional productivity. There is a profound difference between becoming trapped in perpetual busyness and strategically increasing income for a season in order to accelerate freedom for decades.

Many readers will discover that increasing income produces benefits extending well beyond the numbers themselves. Confidence grows when people begin recognizing the value they bring to the marketplace. Skills improve through use. Relationships expand. Opportunities appear that would have remained invisible without movement. The process often reveals capacities that had gone unnoticed for years.

The Montague Method encourages builders to ask a different question than they may have asked previously. Instead of asking only, "How can I spend less?" builders begin asking, "What problems am I capable of solving, and who benefits when I solve them well?" The first question focuses attention on limitation. The second focuses attention on contribution, and contribution has a remarkable tendency to create opportunity.

Not every opportunity deserves pursuit. Some income streams consume more than they create once time, transportation, stress, and family responsibilities are considered honestly. Builders evaluate opportunities the same way they evaluate debt, investments, and commitments of every kind: according to their long-term contribution to the structure being built.

Eventually an important transition begins to occur. Money stops being viewed primarily as something earned through hours and begins being viewed as something created through value. The distinction matters because hours possess natural limits while value can often be multiplied through systems, businesses, investments, teaching, intellectual property, and ownership.

This realization has changed countless families. The individual who learns to exchange labor for income may survive comfortably. The individual who learns to create value at scale begins participating in an entirely different conversation. Builders recognize both approaches as honorable while understanding that one often creates opportunities for ownership, legacy, and generational impact that the other may struggle to sustain.

Debt reduction remains important work.

Income growth remains important work as well.

The households that master both often discover that financial rebuilding begins accelerating with a speed that once seemed impossible, because resources are no longer moving in only one direction. Money is leaving through debt payments, certainly, but new streams are beginning to flow toward the household at the same time. Rivers fill reservoirs much faster than buckets alone.

Chapter Sixteen

Ownership Is Liberation

History teaches many lessons to those willing to listen carefully, but one lesson appears with remarkable consistency across centuries, nations, and cultures: owners experience the world differently than consumers.

The distinction extends beyond income and often beyond wealth itself. Owners think differently about time because they understand the compounding effect of patient stewardship. Owners think differently about communities because they recognize that improving neighborhoods, businesses, schools, and institutions often improves the value of what they have helped to build. Owners think differently about future generations because ownership naturally encourages longer horizons than consumption and invites decisions that may not reveal their full value for decades.

Debt frequently interferes with this transition because income already committed to obligations from the past possesses less capacity to acquire assets for the future. Capital that might have become investments, business ownership, rental property, productive equipment, intellectual property, or entrepreneurial ventures instead becomes committed to purchases that have already disappeared. The issue is not simply the money itself. The issue is the opportunities that money might otherwise have created.

This is one reason debt freedom matters so much. Debt elimination restores options, and options often become the raw materials from which ownership is constructed. The family that once focused exclusively upon surviving the month gradually discovers that entirely different questions have entered the conversation. Resources can now be directed toward investments, business ownership, property acquisition, charitable work, educational opportunities, and assets capable of continuing to produce value long after the original labor has ended. The change is not merely financial. It is philosophical.

Ownership changes the relationship between labor and income because ownership allows effort performed once to continue producing value over time. A rental property may continue generating income long after the renovation work has ended. A business may continue serving customers while the owner sleeps. A book may continue teaching readers decades after it is written. An investment account quietly compounds while attention is directed elsewhere. Ownership allows time itself to become a partner in the building process rather than simply a resource exchanged for wages.

The wisdom traditions have long treated stewardship seriously because stewardship naturally moves toward multiplication. Seeds are planted rather than admired. Land is cultivated rather than merely possessed. Talents are invested rather than buried. Productive assets are expected to produce because creation itself appears designed around growth, cultivation, and increase. Ownership simply extends this principle into economic life by asking resources to continue serving purposes beyond the moment in which they were acquired.

This conversation carries particular significance for the African diaspora because ownership has often been interrupted, delayed, restricted, or actively prevented throughout significant portions of history. Access to land, business ownership, capital, banking relationships, and investment opportunities has not always been distributed evenly or fairly. Acknowledging this history matters because history influences starting positions even when it does not determine destinations.

Builders understand this distinction instinctively. The absence of inherited ownership becomes an invitation to create ownership. The absence of family businesses becomes an opportunity to establish them. The absence of investment culture creates an opportunity to teach it intentionally to children and grandchildren. Communities that lack institutions capable of serving local needs eventually discover that institutions can be built just as surely as homes, businesses, and neighborhoods can be built.

Communities change when ownership changes. A neighborhood that owns grocery stores experiences food access differently than a neighborhood dependent entirely upon outside investment. A community that owns banks experiences capital differently than one dependent exclusively upon outside lenders. A people who own media, schools, businesses, housing, and institutions participate differently in economic life than a people who merely consume what others create. Ownership changes incentives because owners naturally become interested in maintenance, excellence, long-term health, and the prosperity of the surrounding environment.

None of this should be interpreted as hostility toward employment. Employment remains honorable work and has supported millions of successful families. The invitation is simply to expand the conversation. Labor income may provide stability, while ownership often creates leverage and continuity beyond the hours personally worked. The two approaches frequently complement one another beautifully when pursued with intention and discipline.

Eventually the conversation changes once again. The central question is no longer simply how to escape debt but what that freedom was intended to build. Debt reduction creates margin, margin creates options, and options create opportunities for ownership and stewardship that may survive long enough to benefit people the builder will never personally meet. That possibility moves the discussion beyond personal finance and into the realm of legacy.

That is not merely economics.

That is stewardship extended through time.

Chapter Seventeen

A Prosperous Name

There is an interesting question hiding beneath most financial conversations, though it rarely introduces itself immediately. The question is not how much money a person earned, accumulated, invested, or spent. The deeper question is what remains after the person who earned it is no longer present to explain what it meant. Wealth eventually changes hands. Houses change owners. Businesses are sold. Investment accounts are distributed. What survives those transfers often reveals what was actually being built all along.

The wisdom traditions have always treated names seriously because names carry far more than identification. A name gathers reputation, habits, values, expectations, relationships, and memories over time. Businesses spend enormous resources attempting to establish trustworthy names because trust lowers resistance and opens doors that contracts alone often struggle to unlock. Families understand this instinctively. Children inherit stories about who they are, what they are capable of becoming, and what kind of future they should expect long before they inherit money.

A prosperous name therefore extends beyond financial assets. Some families pass along businesses, property, and investments. Others pass along craftsmanship, discipline, education, faith, resilience, generosity, or service to community. Some transfer habits of ownership and stewardship while others unknowingly transfer habits of consumption and reaction. The inheritance itself may not always be intentional, but inheritances are being transferred nevertheless.

This reality helps explain why financial decisions often possess consequences extending far beyond the present moment. A child raised in a household where budgeting, saving, investing, and generosity are discussed openly enters adulthood carrying tools that may remain useful for an entire lifetime. A child who grows up watching businesses being built, properties being acquired, and opportunities being created often approaches economic life differently than a child for whom ownership remained distant or invisible.

The opposite is equally true. Anxiety travels through generations with surprising efficiency. Financial secrecy becomes cultural. Consumption becomes normal. Debt becomes expected. Entire communities occasionally inherit assumptions about money that were formed under circumstances that no longer exist and yet continue influencing decisions long after the original conditions have disappeared. Builders understand that every generation receives a financial story and then decides which chapters deserve continuation and which chapters deserve revision.

For that reason, builders teach intentionally. They explain credit before the first application is signed and investing before the first paycheck arrives. They discuss ownership as something ordinary rather than exceptional and stewardship as a privilege rather than a burden. Financial literacy becomes less an academic subject and more a family language spoken around dinner tables, during car rides, and through ordinary conversations about decisions, opportunities, and priorities.

The wisdom traditions speak frequently about inheritance because inheritance represents stewardship extended beyond a single lifetime. The Torah treats land, family, and responsibility as deeply connected ideas. The Gospels repeatedly emphasize faithful stewardship and the management of resources entrusted for a season rather than possessed permanently. The Quran frequently returns to themes of justice, generosity, responsibility, and care for both family and community.

Across traditions there exists a remarkably consistent understanding that wealth acquires its greatest meaning when it continues serving purposes larger than the individual who first accumulated it.

Extraordinary wealth is not required to participate in legacy building. Families that normalize discipline, stewardship, entrepreneurship, generosity, and ownership often create advantages that compound quietly across generations. A household that ends cycles of financial confusion and replaces them with understanding may alter the trajectory of descendants who have not yet been born. Knowledge, habits, relationships, wisdom, and character frequently survive economic downturns more effectively than portfolios do.

This chapter also invites an uncomfortable but necessary question. If future generations learned everything they know about money exclusively by observing our behavior, what lessons would they carry forward? The question is not intended to produce guilt but awareness, because examples have always been among humanity's most effective teachers. Children listen to instruction, certainly, but they study behavior with far greater attention.

The Montague Method asks builders to think in generations rather than transactions. Decisions are evaluated not only according to immediate comfort but according to long-term consequences. Purchases, investments, businesses, charitable giving, and financial priorities all become part of a larger conversation concerning the kind of family culture being created and the kind of inheritance quietly taking shape beneath ordinary decisions.

Eventually prosperity begins acquiring a richer definition than the marketplace often provides. Money remains useful, but usefulness alone does not make a life prosperous. Prosperity becomes increasingly connected to stewardship, contribution, durability, and service. A prosperous name is not merely remembered fondly after its owner has departed. It continues creating opportunities, transmitting wisdom, and strengthening communities long after the original builder has laid down the tools.

That may be one of the highest forms of wealth a person can leave behind.

Chapter Eighteen

Teaching the Children to Build

Every civilization eventually faces the same question, whether it asks it explicitly or not: how will the next generation learn what the present generation knows? The question matters because knowledge that is not transferred has a peculiar tendency to disappear, requiring each generation to rediscover lessons that should have arrived as inheritance rather than experience.

Financial stewardship follows this pattern closely. Many adults can identify the moment they first signed for credit, opened a bank account, financed a vehicle, or negotiated a salary. Far fewer can identify the moment someone intentionally explained interest, investing, ownership, taxes, insurance, or the difference between assets and liabilities. Too often, financial education arrives through consequences rather than instruction.

Children learn continuously whether adults are teaching intentionally or not. They observe how money is discussed, how stress is managed, how purchases are evaluated, and how generosity is practiced. They notice whether budgets exist, whether plans are made, and whether decisions are driven primarily by impulse or intention. Long before children understand economics, they begin learning financial culture.

This reality places extraordinary influence in the hands of parents, grandparents, mentors, faith communities, and community leaders. Lessons do not require formal classrooms in order to be effective. Grocery stores teach comparison shopping. Family vacations teach budgeting and planning. Businesses teach value creation. Charitable giving teaches stewardship and responsibility toward others. Ordinary life contains remarkable educational opportunities for those willing to recognize them.

The objective is not to raise children who merely avoid debt. The objective is to raise builders. Builders understand delayed gratification because construction projects have always required patience. Builders understand ownership because ownership creates options. Builders understand service because value creation begins with improving life for someone else. Builders understand stewardship because resources that are managed wisely tend to create opportunities for future generations.

The wisdom traditions consistently treat children as investments rather than interruptions. The Torah repeatedly emphasizes teaching principles diligently and integrating them into daily life rather than reserving them for occasional instruction. The Gospels frequently employ agricultural imagery that assumes planting, cultivation, patience, and eventual harvest. The Quran repeatedly returns to responsibility, learning, and preparation for those who will follow behind us. Across traditions there exists an expectation that wisdom should travel intentionally from one generation to the next.

Conversations about money deserve a place within that transfer of wisdom. Children benefit from understanding that every purchase carries an opportunity cost and that every dollar assigned to one purpose becomes unavailable for another. They benefit from learning that credit can be useful and dangerous, that ownership differs from consumption, and that wealth often grows quietly through discipline rather than dramatically through luck.

Entrepreneurship deserves attention as well because entrepreneurship teaches lessons extending far beyond business formation. A child who sells lemonade, cuts grass, tutors classmates, or creates digital products begins learning relationships between effort, value, service, and compensation that are difficult to replicate through theory alone. Markets provide feedback with remarkable honesty, and honest feedback has always been an effective teacher.

The goal is not to pressure children into careers they did not choose or ambitions they do not share. The goal is to introduce tools and possibilities early enough that future choices become expansions rather than discoveries. A young adult encountering investing, ownership, negotiation, and entrepreneurship for the first time at age thirty begins from a different position than one who has heard those conversations around the dinner table since childhood.

Communities play an important role here as well. Children benefit from seeing business owners, investors, skilled tradesmen, educators, healthcare professionals, artists, ministers, and entrepreneurs who look like them and share their experiences. Possibility often becomes easier to believe once it becomes visible. Representation alone does not create outcomes, but invisibility has rarely improved them.

Eventually a generation raised to build begins changing the landscape around it. Businesses appear where none previously existed. Properties are acquired and improved. Institutions emerge. Capital begins circulating differently. Economic conversations become less concerned with survival and increasingly concerned with stewardship, ownership, and contribution.

That transformation rarely begins in boardrooms.

More often it begins around kitchen tables.

And perhaps that is exactly where many revolutions were always supposed to begin.

Chapter Nineteen

The Community Dividend

Every dollar tells a story.

Some dollars enter a community and remain there for years, moving from local businesses to local employees, from local employees to local homeowners, and from local homeowners to local institutions. Other dollars arrive in the morning and leave before sunset, carrying purchasing power, opportunity, and influence elsewhere before returning only long enough to repeat the process again. Builders pay attention to where money travels because money behaves much like water. Communities that retain and direct resources intentionally often experience very different outcomes than communities that function primarily as points of consumption within someone else's economic system.

Individual financial responsibility remains essential, but individuals rarely succeed in isolation. Families depend upon schools, employers, transportation systems, healthcare providers, banks, grocery stores, and local businesses. Every community already participates in an economic ecosystem whether it recognizes that ecosystem or not. The more important question is who owns that ecosystem and who benefits most from its success.

Ownership changes the conversation because ownership changes incentives. A community that participates in the ownership of housing, financial institutions, media companies, businesses, healthcare systems, educational institutions, and productive assets experiences economic life differently than one dependent entirely upon decisions made elsewhere. Ownership encourages maintenance, long-term thinking, excellence, and stewardship because owners naturally become invested in the health of what they have helped to build.

This should not be confused with economic isolation. Trade has always created prosperity by allowing people, businesses, and communities to specialize, exchange value, and benefit from one another's strengths. The objective is not withdrawal from the broader economy but meaningful participation within it. Builders seek partnership without dependency and cooperation without surrendering ownership entirely to outside interests.

The wisdom traditions understood long ago that healthy communities require more than successful individuals. The Torah repeatedly connects economic life to communal responsibility and mutual obligation. The Gospels emphasize stewardship that strengthens neighbors as well as households. The Quran consistently joins prosperity with justice, generosity, and concern for the vulnerable. Across traditions runs a common understanding that economics functions best when it serves people rather than asking people to serve economics.

This conversation carries particular significance for the African diaspora because ownership and access to capital have often been interrupted by historical forces larger than individual households. Communities that were denied opportunities to accumulate assets frequently became exceptionally skilled consumers while being denied equivalent opportunities to become owners at comparable scale. The resulting imbalance was not a shortage of intelligence, discipline, creativity, or ambition. It was largely a shortage of infrastructure and ownership opportunities.

Builders respond to infrastructure problems by building infrastructure. Financial institutions, businesses, investment groups, housing developments, schools, media organizations, and community enterprises do not emerge spontaneously from the landscape. They are planned, financed, organized, and sustained by people willing to think beyond immediate consumption and toward long-term stewardship. The absence of such institutions within a community may explain present realities, but it does not determine future possibilities.

The earliest stages of this work often appear surprisingly modest. Families begin supporting local businesses more intentionally. Investors pool resources to acquire productive assets that would remain inaccessible individually. Mentorship programs emerge for young entrepreneurs. Scholarships are created for future builders. Community organizations begin teaching ownership, investing, and financial literacy with the same seriousness previously reserved for employment preparation. None of these actions changes the world overnight. Taken together over time, they change communities with remarkable consistency.

Eventually children begin growing up in environments where ownership is ordinary rather than exceptional. Business owners become familiar figures rather than distant exceptions. Investment conversations become as normal as conversations about employment. The range of possibilities expands because possibility itself has become visible. Communities often move toward the futures they can imagine, and imagination becomes easier once examples are standing in plain sight.

The Montague Method encourages builders to think beyond the boundaries of individual households because prosperity has always possessed a communal dimension. Families thrive more easily in healthy communities, and healthy communities emerge more naturally when builders begin asking not only what they can earn, but what they can help create. The question slowly shifts from personal survival to collective stewardship, and that shift often marks the beginning of durable change.

The community dividend is simply the return generated when stewardship, ownership, discipline, and long-term thinking begin operating together over extended periods of time. Like most worthwhile investments, the early returns may appear modest to impatient observers. Over generations, however, communities built upon ownership and stewardship often produce results that appear almost inevitable in retrospect, even though they were constructed one decision, one institution, and one family at a time.

Chapter Twenty

The Generosity Principle

Generosity is often misunderstood in financial conversations. Some imagine generosity belongs exclusively to the wealthy, while others treat it as a luxury reserved for some distant season after every obligation has disappeared and every financial goal has been achieved. The result is that generosity becomes permanently postponed, waiting patiently for a future that somehow never quite arrives.

The wisdom traditions offer a different perspective. Generosity is presented not as the reward for stewardship but as one of its expressions. The Torah repeatedly connects prosperity with responsibility toward the widow, the orphan, the stranger, and the poor. The Gospels describe stewardship as something measured not merely by accumulation but by faithfulness and compassion. The Quran consistently joins prosperity with charity, justice, and care for the vulnerable. Across traditions there appears a common understanding that resources acquire greater meaning when they participate in purposes larger than personal consumption.

This principle often feels counterintuitive because scarcity teaches people to hold tightly. A person emerging from financial instability may understandably fear that generosity threatens security and delays recovery. Experience frequently teaches the opposite lesson. Generosity does not require recklessness, nor does stewardship require selfishness. The healthiest financial lives often develop the capacity to protect resources wisely while releasing them purposefully.

Builders approach generosity with intentionality rather than impulse. They understand that generosity extends beyond spontaneous giving and includes the deliberate support of families, communities, institutions, ministries, schools, businesses, and causes that improve the lives of others. The objective is not merely to respond to need but to participate in solutions that reduce need over time.

Generosity also changes the person practicing it. Money has a peculiar ability to migrate from the wallet to the imagination, eventually becoming attached to identity, status, or security in ways that exceed its practical function. Intentional giving interrupts that migration. It reminds the steward that money remains a tool rather than a master and that ownership itself is often temporary stewardship carried out over a particular season of life.

Communities benefit from this principle as well. Scholarships emerge because someone gave. Food programs continue because someone gave. Churches remain open, missions continue operating, entrepreneurs receive encouragement, and families survive difficult seasons because generosity quietly moved through the hands of ordinary people who decided that stewardship involved more than accumulation.

The Montague Method therefore treats generosity not as the enemy of prosperity but as one of its purposes. Debt elimination creates margin. Margin creates options. Options create opportunities for ownership, investment, and service. A healthy financial life eventually discovers that receiving and giving are not opposing forces but complementary movements within the same system of stewardship.

This chapter does not advocate financial irresponsibility disguised as compassion. Builders do not neglect their families in order to appear generous, nor do they create crises at home while solving problems elsewhere. Stewardship requires balance, planning, and wisdom because generosity sustained over decades usually accomplishes more than generosity fueled briefly by emotion alone.

There is another reason generosity matters. It changes the stories communities tell themselves about what is possible. A child who receives a scholarship often remembers the opportunity long after the money itself has been spent. A struggling family remembers the season someone helped carry the burden. A young entrepreneur remembers the person who believed in an idea before the marketplace did. Resources may disappear with use, but the possibilities they create frequently continue multiplying in ways no spreadsheet could ever fully capture.

Eventually prosperity begins to feel less like possession and more like participation. The steward recognizes that resources arrive carrying assignments and opportunities as well as benefits. At that point generosity no longer feels like subtraction from the balance sheet. It feels more like an investment in people, communities, and futures that may continue producing returns long after the original giver has finished counting them.

Perhaps that is why generosity has survived in the wisdom traditions for thousands of years. It strengthens communities, protects the humanity of the steward, and reminds builders that the highest forms of wealth have always been measured by more than what was kept.

Chapter Twenty-One

Rebuilding the Prosperous Name

There comes a moment in many rebuilding stories when the numbers stop being the most interesting part of the conversation. Balances have fallen. Savings have grown. Credit has improved. Systems are functioning. Plans exist where uncertainty once lived. Somewhere along the journey, the builder realizes that the real construction project was never limited to finances alone. Money may have provided the measurements, but character supplied the materials from which the new structure was ultimately built.

Debt has a peculiar habit of shrinking horizons. Immediate obligations crowd out important questions because due dates demand attention while dreams generally wait patiently in the background. A person carrying enough financial pressure can spend years responding to emergencies without noticing that emergencies have quietly become a lifestyle. Rebuilding interrupts this pattern by creating room for longer thoughts, larger goals, and conversations that extend beyond the end of the month.

One of the first questions to emerge from that space is surprisingly simple: what kind of person handles money well? The answer rarely begins with spreadsheets or investment accounts. Financial stewardship draws heavily from qualities that were valuable long before banks, credit reports, and credit cards existed. Discipline matters. Patience matters. Honesty matters. Reliability matters. Communities have trusted such people with responsibility for thousands of years because responsibility has always flowed naturally toward those who demonstrate readiness for it.

An interesting reversal begins occurring as these qualities shape financial behavior. Stewardship starts strengthening the very character traits that made stewardship possible in the first place. Discipline grows stronger through use. Patience becomes more natural through practice. Confidence develops through evidence rather than optimism alone. The builder slowly becomes the kind of person capable of carrying larger responsibilities because smaller responsibilities were carried faithfully first.

This is one reason the prosperous name matters so much. A prosperous name is not merely admired; it becomes useful. Banks extend trust more easily to people who honor commitments consistently. Business partners seek reliability. Communities look for wisdom and stability during uncertain seasons. Opportunities frequently travel along relational pathways, and relationships have always depended heavily upon trust.

The wisdom traditions understood this principle long before economists attempted to quantify it. A good name was treated as an asset because trust lowers friction wherever human beings cooperate. Merchants understood it in marketplaces. Families understood it around dinner tables. Communities understood it in moments of crisis and opportunity alike. The principle survived because experience continued proving it true.

This conversation carries particular significance for the African diaspora because history has often required extraordinary resilience merely to preserve opportunities that others inherited automatically. Rebuilding the prosperous name therefore involves more than individual advancement. It includes restoring stories interrupted by discrimination, exclusion, displacement, and lost opportunities while simultaneously creating new stories that future generations may inherit intact.

Builders participate in this restoration every time they honor agreements, teach stewardship, mentor younger leaders, support local institutions, create opportunities for others, and approach ownership as a responsibility rather than merely a privilege. The work often appears modest while it is occurring because important construction projects rarely announce their significance while foundations are being poured. Time, however, has always possessed a remarkable capacity for multiplication.

Eventually the builder notices another change taking place. Financial decisions no longer feel isolated from spiritual decisions, family decisions, leadership decisions, or community decisions because stewardship has a way of connecting rooms that once appeared unrelated. The habits that create trustworthy financial behavior often create trustworthy leadership, trustworthy friendships, trustworthy families, and trustworthy institutions as well.

The objective of stewardship was never perfection because perfection has never been among humanity's available options. The deeper objective is alignment, the gradual process through which values and behavior begin recognizing one another again and fewer resources are spent maintaining contradictions between belief and practice. That quiet consistency often becomes one of the most valuable forms of prosperity available to any human being.

Prosperous names are rarely built through dramatic moments or singular achievements. They emerge through thousands of decisions, habits, conversations, promises kept, and responsibilities honored when no audience is present and no applause is available. Over time those ordinary moments accumulate into reputations, and reputations occasionally become inheritances that continue opening doors for people the original builder may never personally meet. That is how prosperous names travel through time.

Chapter Twenty-Two

The Doors Were Never Locked

The strange thing about modern debtors' prison is that the doors are often unlocked, and yet millions of people still feel unable to leave.

The feeling is understandable. Debt changes the relationship between labor and time because future income begins arriving with obligations already attached to it. Choices become narrower. Possibilities become quieter. Entire households can spend years making decisions based less upon values, opportunities, and aspirations than upon agreements made months or years earlier. Given enough time, those limitations can begin feeling permanent even when they are not.

Some eventually conclude that this arrangement is simply adulthood. Debt becomes normal. Financial anxiety becomes normal. Living paycheck to paycheck becomes normal. Communities occasionally inherit assumptions about money that were developed during emergencies and quietly transformed into expectations. The prison becomes most effective when the people living inside it stop imagining life beyond its walls.

The purpose of this book was never merely debt elimination, important though debt elimination may be. Credit repair matters because trust matters. Ownership matters because ownership creates options. Stewardship matters because resources behave differently when given purpose and direction. Community matters because individuals rarely thrive for long in unhealthy environments. Beneath each of these conversations, however, lay a deeper question concerning identity and the stories people tell themselves about what is possible.

Builders answer that question differently.

Builders understand that measurements describe locations rather than destinies. They tell themselves the truth about present conditions without surrendering to those conditions as permanent definitions of who they are. They recognize that difficult seasons require honesty, discipline, patience, and courage, but they also recognize that none of those seasons possesses authority over what may eventually be built next.

Along the journey another truth quietly emerged. Financial rebuilding was never solely about money because money touches almost every other room in the house. It influences marriages, health, opportunities, ministries, businesses, neighborhoods, and futures not yet born. Stewardship therefore became larger than budgeting, and prosperity became larger than accumulation. By the end of the conversation the focus had expanded to include ownership, legacy, generosity, family culture, and institutions capable of serving communities for generations.

That expansion matters because freedom without purpose rarely survives for long. Empty spaces have a remarkable tendency to refill themselves with old habits wearing new clothes. Builders therefore require projects worthy of their freedom. Some will build businesses. Others will build ministries, schools, scholarships, investment groups, mentoring programs, or institutions capable of serving communities long after the original builders have laid down their tools. The specific assignment matters less than the decision to build intentionally.

The wisdom traditions consistently remind humanity that stewardship is temporary and responsibility is real. The Torah teaches responsibility across generations and the faithful management of resources entrusted to human hands. The Gospels repeatedly return to themes of stewardship, multiplication, and accountability. The Quran consistently joins prosperity with justice, generosity, and responsibility toward family and community. Across traditions there remains a common understanding that wealth acquires its deepest meaning when it participates in purposes larger than the individual who first possessed it.

Eventually the builder notices something unexpected. The prison that once appeared immovable begins looking very different from the outside than it looked from within. The walls were real, the burdens were real, and the fear was real as well. Yet possibilities existed throughout the journey that could not always be seen from inside the fog of obligation and uncertainty. Perspective changes many things, and one of the things it changes is the apparent size of the walls.

Some readers will finish this book carrying substantial debt, rebuilding damaged credit, or recovering from foreclosure, unemployment, illness, divorce, or financial decisions that continue casting long shadows. None of those realities determines the identity of the builder because builders are not defined by the stage of construction they currently occupy. They are defined by their willingness to continue building despite the stage they occupy.

The work now belongs to the reader. Builders begin where they are rather than where they wish they were. They begin with the end in mind, tell themselves the truth about present conditions, and continue building patiently enough for discipline to become momentum and momentum to become transformation. Freedom, once reclaimed, deserves construction projects worthy of its arrival.

One day, perhaps sooner than seems possible from where you stand today, you may find yourself looking back at roads that once appeared impossible to travel and distances that once appeared impossible to cross. When that day arrives, take a moment to appreciate what has happened. The circumstances may not have changed all at once, and the work may not have felt dramatic while it was occurring. Nevertheless, a builder emerged from the journey stronger, wiser, and more capable than the person who first opened these pages.

The prison did not disappear.

The builder emerged.

And once the builder emerges, the doors begin looking very different indeed.

APPENDIX

Appendix A

Financial Inventory Worksheet

The Montague Method begins with truth.

Builders measure before they build, inspect before they repair, and inventory before they invest resources. Financial anxiety often grows in environments where information is incomplete, scattered, or avoided altogether. This worksheet is designed to replace uncertainty with clarity and provide an accurate picture of your current position.

Income Sources

List every source of household income.

Source	Monthly Amount
Employment Income	
Spouse Income	
Pension	
Disability Compensation	
Social Security	
Business Income	
Rental Income	
Investment Income	
Other Income	

Total Monthly Income: __________

Monthly Obligations

Expense Category	Monthly Amount
Housing	
Utilities	
Transportation	
Insurance	
Food	
Healthcare	
Childcare	
Debt Payments	
Savings	
Other	

Total Monthly Expenses: __________

Debt Inventory

Creditor	Balance	Interest Rate	Minimum Payment

Assets Inventory

Asset	Estimated Value
Checking Accounts	
Savings Accounts	
Retirement Accounts	
Real Estate	
Vehicles	
Business Interests	
Investments	
Other Assets	

Immediate Threat Assessment

Are you currently facing:

- Foreclosure
- Eviction
- Utility Disconnection
- Repossession
- Food Insecurity
- Medical Crisis
- Income Loss

If yes, identify the issue and timeline:

Builder's Assessment

What is the most important financial issue requiring attention during the next thirty days?

What is the single most important financial objective for the next twelve months?

Appendix B

Debt Elimination Planner

Debt elimination is rarely an event.

It is usually a sequence of decisions repeated consistently over time.

Debt Priority Worksheet

Creditor	Balance	Interest Rate	Minimum Payment	Priority Ranking

Strategy Selection

Choose your primary strategy:

□ Snowball Method

□ Avalanche Method

□ Hybrid Method

□ Custom Strategy

Why did you choose this approach?

Target Payoff Schedule

Debt	Target Payoff Date

Additional Payment Opportunities

Potential sources of accelerated payments:

- Tax refunds
- Bonuses
- Overtime income
- Sale of unused assets
- Side income
- Gifts
- Reduced discretionary spending

What additional monthly amount can be directed toward debt reduction?

$__________________

Milestone Tracker

Milestone	Completion Date
First Debt Eliminated	
25% Reduction Achieved	
50% Reduction Achieved	
75% Reduction Achieved	
Debt Freedom Achieved	

Reflection

What opportunities will become available when these obligations no longer exist?

What will your freedom build?

Appendix C

Credit Repair Checklist and Dispute Tracker

Credit reports are historical records.

They are not identities, verdicts, or prophecies.

Builders review records carefully because decisions improve when information improves.

Credit Report Review

Date reports obtained:

-
-
-

Credit bureaus reviewed:

□ Equifax

□ Experian

□ TransUnion

Potential Errors Identified

□ Incorrect personal information

□ Duplicate accounts

- ☐ Incorrect balances
- ☐ Incorrect payment history
- ☐ Accounts not belonging to me
- ☐ Obsolete information
- ☐ Incorrect collection accounts
- ☐ Incorrect public records

Dispute Tracking Log

Item Disputed	Bureau	Date Submitted	Status

Documentation Checklist

- ☐ Credit report copies
- ☐ Supporting statements
- ☐ Payment records
- ☐ Identity verification
- ☐ Correspondence copies

□ Certified mail receipts

Follow-Up Schedule

Date	Action Required

Builder's Reflection

What lesson has this process taught you about stewardship, recordkeeping, and financial organization?

How will you protect your financial reputation moving forward?

Appendix D

Collection Communication Log

Prepared people communicate differently than frightened people.

The purpose of this log is not confrontation. It is clarity. Good records reduce confusion, preserve important details, and improve decision making during difficult seasons. Builders document conversations because memory fades while records endure.

Creditor and Collector Directory

Organization	Contact Person	Phone Number	Account Number

Communication Log

Date	Time	Organiza-tion	Represen-tative	Summary of Conversation	Next Action

Documentation Received

Date Received	Document Description	Action Required

Payment Agreements

Organization	Agreement Terms	Due Date	Status

Builder's Notes

What information became clearer through documentation?

What questions remain unanswered?

What is the next best action available to you?

Reminder

Professional communication, accurate records, and timely follow-up often improve outcomes significantly. Builders do not surrender agency during difficult conversations. They prepare, document, verify, and proceed with clarity.

Appendix E

Emergency Financial Stabilization Worksheet

Some builders begin with blueprints.

Others begin in the middle of a storm.

This worksheet is designed for immediate stabilization during periods of financial crisis. The objective is not perfection. The objective is preserving people, shelter, income, and the possibility of rebuilding.

Immediate Threat Assessment

Check all that apply:

□ Foreclosure

□ Eviction

□ Utility Disconnection

□ Repossession

□ Food Insecurity

□ Loss of Employment

□ Medical Emergency

□ Transportation Crisis

□ Other: ____________________

Housing Status

Current housing situation:

Critical deadlines:

Actions required within the next seven days:

Income Protection

Current income sources:

Potential income interruptions:

Actions required to preserve income:

Food Security Assessment

Current concerns:

Available resources:

Immediate actions:

Transportation Assessment

Current transportation situation:

Risk factors:

Stabilization actions:

Support Network Inventory

Family members who may assist:

Faith community resources:

Community organizations:

Government programs:

Veteran resources:

Thirty-Day Stabilization Plan

Priority	Action	Deadline
1		
2		
3		
4		
5		

Builder's Reflection

What is the most important issue requiring immediate attention?

What resources are available that have not yet been explored?

What is the next best decision available today?

Reminder

Financial emergencies create urgency, but urgency is not permission for panic. Builders preserve what matters most, protect the foundation, and make decisions from information rather than fear.

Appendix F

Ownership and Legacy Planner

Debt freedom is not the destination.

It is the runway.

The purpose of this planner is to help builders begin directing freedom toward ownership, stewardship, and legacy.

Ownership Vision

What does ownership mean to you and your family?

What assets would you like your family to own within the next ten years?

Ownership Goals

Check all that apply:

□ Home Ownership

□ Business Ownership

□ Investment Accounts

□ Rental Property

□ Intellectual Property

□ Community Investment Projects

□ Agricultural Assets

□ Other: ____________________

Business and Value Creation

What problems are you capable of solving for others?

What skills, experience, or expertise possess market value?

What opportunities deserve further exploration?

Legacy Planning

What values do you want future generations to inherit?

What financial lessons should be taught intentionally?

What family traditions should continue?

Community Stewardship

How can your success contribute to the health of your community?

What institutions would you like to help build or strengthen?

What opportunities can you create for others?

The Prosperous Name Statement

Complete the following sentence:

"Our family will be known for…"

The Builder's Commitment

I commit myself to stewardship, ownership, service, generosity, and disciplined construction. I understand that prosperity extends beyond accumulation and includes responsibility toward family, community, and generations yet unborn.

Signature: ______________________________

Date: __________________________________

About the Author

Aaron Maxwell Montague, MBA, M.Div., MNLP, MTT, MCHt, MSC is an author, educator, coach, minister, and community builder whose life's work is centered on helping individuals and communities reclaim purpose, strengthen stewardship, and build lasting legacies. A retired United States Navy Master Training Specialist and disabled veteran, Aaron also dedicated more than two decades to serving fellow veterans as a National Appeals Officer Supervisor with the Disabled American Veterans (DAV), advocating on behalf of those who served our nation.

Aaron serves as Associate Pastor at Kingdom Celebration Center in Gambrills, Maryland, where his ministry emphasizes biblical stewardship, discipleship, leadership development, and practical faith. He is also the founder of MX3 Motivational Ministries and MX3 Motivational Books, organizations committed to equipping people to grow spiritually, intellectually, financially, and personally.

Holding graduate degrees in business and divinity, along with advanced certifications in Neuro-Linguistic Programming, clinical hypnotherapy, coaching, and training, Aaron brings together insights from leadership, behavioral science, economics, theology, and education to help readers move beyond information toward meaningful transformation. His writing is distinguished by the Montague Method, a philosophy that combines thoughtful reflection, practical application, and disciplined action to help readers become builders of prosperous lives, families, and communities.

Aaron is the author of several books, including T*he West Philadelphia Billionaire Society, Not Who We Are, Money Moves, The Mirror, 2029, 31 Days of Wisdom, As a Mind Thinketh, and Speaking Health Into Existence.* His work consistently explores the themes of identity, ownership, stewardship, leadership, and the restoration of individuals and communities through education and purposeful action.

In Breaking Out of Debtors' Prison, Aaron draws upon decades of experience in ministry, coaching, financial education, leadership, and public service to present a practical roadmap for eliminating debt, repairing financial identity, building ownership, and creating a prosperous name capable of blessing generations yet unborn. His vision extends beyond personal financial success to the development of families, institutions, and communities characterized by stewardship, responsibility, and opportunity.

Aaron and his wife, Wanda, are passionate advocates for lifelong learning, community development, and empowering others to build lives marked by faith, wisdom, generosity, and enduring legacy.

To learn more about Aaron's books, speaking engagements, coaching, and educational resources, visit **MX3MotivationalBooks.com**.